ADAM'S RIB

Poetry in Her Honor

Jules Ryu Pierre

ADAM'S RIB

By Jules Ryu Pierre

ISBN 978-0-578-17693-2

This book is dedicated :

To man's other half, for without her-Adam is incomplete.

To the muses who have inspired these words over the years.

To my Cruzan sisters Candyce & Portia who motivated me to birth this project.

To my sisters at home, Lorette & Sandra who've had my back since day one-Love you both.

To my brother-in-law Patrick who believed a writer's pipe dream.

Last but not least, to the God who breathed life into my soul & my pen. To Him who blessed me with

the woman of God who raised me & exhibited the meaning of true strength & beauty…

Pour Gisele: Mesi anpil cheri.

Genesis 2

21So the LORD God caused a deep sleep to fall upon the man, and he slept; then He took one of his ribs and closed up the flesh at that place.22The LORD God fashioned into a woman the rib which He had taken from the man, and brought her to the man. 23The man said, "This is now bone of my bones, And flesh of my flesh; She shall be called Woman, Because she was taken out of Man."…

I love the way she bends   with the wind at her back

She is ten paces before time-

She is powerful, masterful at breathing mayhem into existence & changing our opinions of women.

I, poetically inclined to speak for mute men declare our reverence

Pay careful attention to the way she moves- conflict attempting to capture her spirit- but she is not your average victim

Baptized by fire, floods, & liars—Behold the crux   of my desire.

Chapter 1: Solomon's Songs

Song of Solomon 4:4

Your neck is like the tower of David, built with courses of stone;

on it hang a thousand shields, all of them shields of warriors.

Song of Solomon 7:8

I said, "I will climb the palm tree; I will take hold of its fruit." May your breasts be like clusters of grapes on the vine, the

fragrance of your breath like apples, and your mouth like the best wine.

Celebration

Your body amazes me
      Though I have seen it a thousand times
          in dreams
          and in days
     I continue to be *caught*
          in a state of appreciation
    from the curve of your spine to
          the lean in your form
          the tilt of your hips
          to the shape of your jaw

Yes, I am that mad scientist
      Who explores his subject
      toe to head   pen in hand
          face to glass
      I wish to learn all there is
          about this creature
          from how she breathes
          to how to please her
      True, parts of me are at attention
          when I witness her in natural form
          but no, my admiration is not limited
             to this one charm
      It is her ora   her femininity
          sex appeal
    agility in movement and
          so much more…
    I do appreciate her sensitivity
          which cancels out my brutish ways
    Her willingness to try when I am fearful
          I may fail

    This must be what is meant
          by she completes me
    Apparently, Adam's rib   was very well spent.

You're so easy

I write poems about you

in my sleep

I dream & just as it's

About to get deep

You slip into focus

Before my camera lens

In   out

Then back again

The eighth wonder of the world

20,000 leagues into the deep blue sea

30,000 feet up in air

I stare thru the window into

God's living quarters

And Heaven is just as I pictured

Incredible   surreal

And incomplete   cause you're not there

But here on Earth on Sabbatical

What a radical notion….

But no dear reader,

This poem was not rehearsed

It was formed in one quick breath

As I exhaled

it fell

      onto

            the page

               freely

Like Icarus falling from sick ambition

I have this vision that has just occurred in one swift blur

It is you in my mind as I close my eyes

Into the netherworld......

I open my eyes

Yet Icarus

      Continues

            to

               Fall

Jules 4 The Queen

And with this poem   I will make her *immortal…*

Men shall see her centuries from now in these words,
Details   exhaled from the tip of my pen   depicting her ora

Crazy Sexy   Muse.

Yet the enigma she'll remain

I have sketched her   the Atlas waiting to be deciphered

Point by point   I will direct   they shall navigate,

But never reach my destination

You see,

She Is poetry

A body of similes & metaphors intertwined

Passed down from a lineage of Queens- Brand Nubian I mean

Reminiscent of an Egyptian seductress

Confident in speech, movement, charm

Grace emanating from her pores like honey
falling from a beehive

She Is symmetry
the defining lines of the story

without which, there is no beginning   ending

Or climax..

But how do I say this in words…?

How do I convey this on the page

without defacing everything God has already created?..

I got it. I will change her to fiction.

Everyone craves fantasy

& in the fantastical realm I can conjure up anything I want-

& not be accused of lying or   exaggerating facts.

So, from now on Babygirl,

Between you & I

You are no longer reality,

But a figment…

of my mind.

Rain Dance

Rain   kisses her cheeks in the morning

Fresh   honey-dipped lips quiver in unison

Floodgates open and I am open to

Say what is on my mind

A pocket full of verses fall

From my mouth to the ground before her

And begins   like

this,

Listen Slim-you are the

Catalyst that makes Him

Tear up

And bless us with

These waters

Fresh

These waters

Yes

These waters

Replenish and rejuvenate us

Like bathing in

A fountain that

Strokes your skin

So softly

You're tempted to

Flip and spin

Like a Taz-maniac

Caught up in a whirlwind

Caught up in this thing that is urging

you to bleed passion from within

the most natural of sins

This   is the stuff that men's dreams are made of

Imperfect women with perfect dimensions

who capture our full attention- span the globe

and you'll find a host who can produce these hallucinations

here a church with no denominations and nothing but temptation

Seek out that vast illusion of contentment

Approach and ask with strong conviction,

Lady of Divine Connections,

May I

Have This Dance?

Nt ur avrg junkie

whn work gets tedious... I wander.....

 The only drug I've ever needed
came straight from her lips
Salvation   @the tip of her tongue
After being stung by the bee I was
left wanting 4more
Jaw wide open as she walked towards the door

I wonder...why do addicts crave meth, coke,
& the symbiotic presence of illmatic pains
when there's so much more we can get high on? Morph into kites n disappear 4a minute..

The confusion is mutual, she says.
I get high off your caramel complexion
your manly essence in acquiescence
to my Queen Bee status- at times erratic-
but never lacking, & emphatically boasting of finer thngs 2come-
& speaking of coming,
Did I ever tell you that when you walk n my direction-
my mind goes backwards n girlish jubilee?
 A childish state I thought was lost..

This is the next level, I interrupted,
where the crux of my existence
exists between your life & how high
my vision can take us
make us greater than we ever imagined-
smoking passion 4brkfst   then askin 4seconds--
w/ a side order of "Daaammn, that's Hot!"

...& then we fall back...

to Earth & chill w/ the "regular people"
who knw not wht we share,
cuz if they did-their jealousy
would wreck our good frtune so quickly   our heads wld roll...

so whaddya say   we just keep
ths little addiction
 as   our little secret?

Trophy

Lady Narcissus takes her usual stance at my dresser

her reflection looking back at me as she admires herself

every once in a while wiping the glass to perfect the image

She cracks a smile

& light particles bounce off the refractive wall

straight into my eyes

I'm nearly blinded by her pearly whites

and no those "hips don't lie"

they tell the story of a woman

who has lived in the gym cultivating curves

and sculpting a piece of ass Rembrandt

would be jealous of

White gloved hands she models to exhibit sophistication

as a compliment to the silky black evening gown (makes her "look slimmer")

that exposes the back of her neck

and reveals the *Princess* tattoo she got *me*

as a birthday present

Forget dime-piece, baby you are   solid gold

But like my childhood trophies

this is getting way too old

you   absorbed in self and immersed

in the wealth of shadows brows and domination

of lipstick over chap stick

I need the warmth of a woman

who lives off the touch of her man

a dame who sees herself in the eyes of her lover

not just before the mirror she stands

I need more than a trophy

I need a partner in crime

a Bonnie to my Clyde

who won't run and hide

when the rain starts to pour (for fear her makeup will run)

I need a princess who's a warrior

not a mere courier for cosmetics in a fifty cent jar

Lady I need a mind that can keep up

with these words that I'm spinnin'

a smart "chick"

quick to understand

slow to complain

and I'll refrain from using those "big words"

you seem to be so terrified of

and to answer your question,

yes

I do still love you

but that's besides the point

the point is

you love you

so much

you no longer

need me.

The XY Equation

X: whats up?

Y: the night sky baby.

X: lol

Y: always

so, how's about you n i traverse the forces of nature n venture up n away for a journey of epic proportions...

you can serve me a portion n i could serve up a passion   n we can imagine ourselves   spinning in flight thru midair...like eagles

my fingers   your hair

X: keep going

Y: your body my hands   ...n we can expand upon the geometric symmetry of the stars in the universe our purse would be the sun awaiting our finale b4 it rears its head.....after we bed, b4 we sleep keeping in tune 2the deep reaches of the galaxy.......it's a mystery, but only we would solve the equation.....a quick computation.....u & i = exceptional math.

She imprisons me with her words

my competition is fierce

rearing the world in the span of her hips

always a welcomed interruption when her lips part

& out depart the words of a philosophical genius

& girl I   mean this when I say you are

Beautifully erotic

the gin to this here tonic

the chronic that I wanna puff puff   & pass on to no man under the
sun

for this is a most selfish affair

I want us to be one

conjoined like Siamese twins hinged so deep in the recesses of each
other's thoughts that we are sharing thought processes

I said

She imprisons me with her words

the absurdity of it all is that I am a lyricist

who builds phrases for a living

& ironically

she uses this same element   to confine my movement

So now, I will bless the Muse….

The Muse:

*Art lovers everywhere adore her   Her image inspires calculated
brushstrokes via urban Michelangelo's*

From the contours of her profile they siphon modern Mona Lisa's

*The romance is in her smile   there is grace in her demeanor, she is The
Muse.*

Politicians cheat on taxes just to access the hyped vixen   Bigoted
men

High spirited men   Inhibited men   All change

Rearrange their theories & miscalculated hyperboles   Just for this
exception

Run interference against gods & principalities in hopes

Of making her acquaintance….Wouldn't that be quaint

Picture this: The flawed man sitting beside the ideal woman

Practically arm & arm attempting to charm her socks &…   top off

But she is *The Muse*   not easily swayed   Calming storms across the
globe

Asserting peace as wars unfold   You wouldn't know it

But her reach is never-ending   Superseding competing
philosophies & causing catastrophes among

Lesser women   Lest they know their place & that they could
never compete against such a

feat as God's *right hand…woman*   For she is *The Muse*   The
pedestal   Heightening the

suspense of men's aspirations for an ass that's worth aspiring

Yes, indeed   she is inspiring

Giving dictation to poets, artists, singers   & making believers out of atheists

Indeed, they shall kneel before this goddess   For she is   The Muse.

Holding the world in the palms of my hands I turned & looked at you

Scores of wealth   My kingdom towers

Yet you I have not

This world alone it just won't do

Delirious (In these Hands)

In these hands exist a malady/ crushing me/ripping through my veins like paper shredding through swift blades

A desire that is crucial   forcing its volition to be heard

Amongst the living who are loving, but lacking   to an infinite degree

In these hands I have strength for the both of us

Unwavering   Uncompromising   Unbreakable

Making fables out of love stories told to young & old

The real depiction shall be exposed in clear poetic vision

Demonstrating the vibration of the heart that is incessantly spiritual

Criminal-minded in wanting to kidnap your being & fleeing to an undisclosed location

In these hands I hold no doubts

No mistresses or reservations

Just plans to woo & subdue your yearnings in a trance/melodic
inclinations of palms denting your backside/hips facing your front side
& me so deep in your inside/dark curtains are a must.

These hands hold the future that is breathing new life in me each &
every day

Holding me captive among clown-like spectators

Laughing at my joy/upon hearing the mention of your name

Cause I'm Delirious   Furiously in love w/the sheer fact of your
existence

In these hands there lies a reckoning of grave danger

The threat of true emotions   slipping into the wrong hands

Being wrongly handled & dismantled

Before the true message reaches the right recipient.

In these hands there are no lies   no games

Just foreplay & plenty of foresight to foresee

Me holding a woman/ whom I truly love.

Excerpt from Mulattre/Mulatto:

She says, "Ohhh he got that…   Good hair. That, Coolie-Miami
Vice-Slash- his momma got down with a light skinned brotha- type
hair. I wanna have your babies, so they too can have that good hair."

But he thinks, "Black woman, you were fashioned by the same genius
who formulated the skies, thought to paint the clouds so they could
rain   down   on   earth...

& from roots form the very plants that would beautify the lands

Then came His angel dust & *poooff*…from the insight of His lens came
the bend of your nose, fullness of lips & cheekbones which compliment
your hue- the very essence of you…So how dare you say you wanna
have my babies   Maybe I, would like to have yours."

Chapter 2: Black, Like the Son

Awake the defiant Black Rose/Touched by Heat/ Light of the Sun Strikes

down & gives breath to a rebel/ out of the Earth is birthed a phenomenal

form/Born is the Queen/ a most spectacular feat/she beats any flower in

the midst of this field/Rebel with a cause/ to show her difference is

worthy/ she dares any to defile & try to counter her glory/ Most High

granted/ Let no man stand in the way of neither brilliance nor power/

Look at me, she says, know that I am strong, proud, & without a doubt

the most vibrant child the ground has ever gifted to the Earth.

Black Diamond

Inspired by the coils of her braided hair

I sat at my desk to write

To nullify all the urban myths

That black was inferior to white.

Her skin was flawless, I thought, as the Nubian goddess disrobed &

    silk fell to the marbled floor

Her moist   parted lips were full   inviting   just as the clever God had

intended

Upended the earth in portions of passion

    spent wakeless hours *shifting* & *bending* his clay to perfection

I directed my eyes across her frame

her nipples/her navel/

the dark vortex of womanhood below…

Then admired the ingenuity of the calculated artist   who crafted a sculpture just the

right measure to satiate a man's appetite   *just right*

I gulped at my intentions   quenching my thirst from the sea of possibilities b4 me

Her hips, wide smile, & captivating brown eyes left me mesmerized

drawing me in to the very depths of my weakness- I speak this as if I'd never seen   a woman like this b4

But this was more than just a chemical reaction

Rather it came like a natural attachment   *borne out of a need for completion*

My rib   her thigh

Her scent   my pores

dying to bleed out to connect to the air she breathed

I heaved a silent sigh

as we prepared to awaken our ancestors to the   ancestral

ceremony

Of ecstasy & necessity   *that bound one to another*

She, strong like her mother

Me, proud like my father

We dissolved   careless   carefree

Muscles undoing chains   voices belying tears   that had formed over

years of unquestioned logic   both tragic & catastrophic

But, I say   Her skin was flawless

& every spec I inspected-though flawed & affected-were perfect, just

like her Mothers.

My mind   in circles, flirting with the purple haze of woman before me--
She's so alluring...like   Cleopatra- Halle Berry- Nefertiti-   but none, like she

They say she's made of Caribbean properties & has African Roots as deep as they be
(Maybe that's why she's so strong)

Battle scars unseen/ she's been wounded in passage/ enslaved- in chains/ yet still
remains...   Beautiful.

From Black Diamond-English/Creole Version

I have searched the four corners of the Earth and have found her essence

She is Beauty   She is Queen She is   the Black Diamond.

They call her   Femme Haitenne. Li si telman bel yo rele'l renn sou la terre, maman ki bay vi. Tande bien, li mete men sou ren'l epi kon'l vire, li dirije aksyon lom. I said, she puts her hands on her hips-tilts, sways & men obey.

Her skin   was flawless I thought, as the Nubian goddess disrobed & silk fell to the marbled floor. Her moist, parted lips were full   inviting   just as the clever God had intended   upended the Earth in portions of passion   Spent wakeless hours shifting & bending his clay to perfection. I directed my eyes along her frame *zepol li   lonbrit li* the dark vortex of womanhood below. Then admired the ingenuity of the calculated artist who crafted a sculpture just the right measure   to satiate a man's appetite. Just right.

Then she stopped and turned to me. Nom mouin se Natalie li di. Enchante. Li fon sou ri, et chenet li paret. Tou boute'l komanse danse…mouin mem, prêt poum tranble.

I gulped at my intentions   quenching my thirst from the sea of possibilities before me.

Her hips, wide smile, & captivating brown eyes *–ket li gen bel je* -left me mesmerized

drawing me in to the very depths of my weakness- I speak this as if I'd never seen   a woman like this b4

This was more than just a chemical reaction

Rather it came like a natural attachment   *borne out of a need for completion*

My rib   her thigh

Her scent   my pores

    dying to bleed out to connect to the air she breathed

I heaved a silent sigh as we prepared to awaken our ancestors to the ancestral ceremony

    Of ecstasy & necessity   *that bound one to another*

She, strong like her mother

Me, proud like my father

We dissolved   careless   carefree

Muscles undoing chains   voices belying tears   that had formed over years of unquestioned logic   both tragic & catastrophic

I say   Her skin was flawless & every spec I inspected-though flawed & affected-were perfect,   Just like her Mothers.

Song of Solomon 1

5 Dark am I, yet lovely,

daughters of Jerusalem,

dark like the tents of Kedar,

like the tent curtains of

Solomon.

6 Do not stare at me

because I am dark,

because I am darkened by the sun.

My mother's sons were

angry with me

and made me take care of

the vineyards;

my own vineyard I had to

neglect.

Black Woman

If only you knew…

How the movement of your lips

made men stutter

Thought processes retarded

by the scope of what stood before them

If only you knew…

How we envied your patience

in times of storms

How your strength was contagious

Calm amazed us

when we

were fit to raise hell

If only you knew…

How we spend all our lives boosting ourselves

just to live up to the worth

of your essence

presence so commanding—we demand

more of ourselves than you

could ever ask

If only you knew…

The Six Train

I inhaled her presence with quick palpitations

beats pounding with breaths I captured her ora

Sage, calm   unphased by the world around her

Hair crowned in braids that drifted to natural

an unsaturated flair about her that

distinguished beauty from fiction

What's her addiction?, I thought

besides the book she reads with such intense concentration…

I inhaled her softly, quietly that is

secluded in my own corner of the train

dissecting her features- the evil mad scientist

struggling to be good—better

yet failing miserably with each new detail acquired

I pondered her thoughts & the awkwardness

of my mutt state before her ebony stature

chocolate-coated/ Heaven's soldiers fight for her well being

and me/ being this close

is only a matter of chance

Can I, romance this vixen

& set a new course for this train?

Perhaps reset the tide & morph myself into

the book she wishes to read… the seed implanted in her thoughts as she flips thru abstract pages..

Or, maybe   I should just start by asking her name.

"Shai Girl"

'The very first time
That I saw your brown eyes
Your lips said "Hello"
And I said "Hi"

I knew right then you were the one
But I was caught up
In physical attraction
But to my satisfaction
*Baby you were more than just a phase'**

She was   more than just a phase,

brown skin, brown eyes,

and I   was left levitating on thin air

Caught   in a state of spatial disorientation of great proportions and proceeding with caution   was the last thing on my mind.

You see, the abstract motion of hips and thighs

caught the attention of these two wandering eyes…..my measuring tape holding her to the highest caliber.

X marks the spot of where you'll find me imbedded- between her lips, between her thoughts,

Between her…

Her tongue in groove with the very makings of my mind & our minds making matters meaningless at that moment in time

Her beauty confounds me, leaving my head pounding like bullets blasting in war time

But this   was a very different type of war

Attacking my senses from every different angle

And then you touched me   Popping my collar & opening my airwaves

Allowing me to breathe again

Mother to my unborn child   This is so damn wild..........

For she   is the poetry of the sages

Fire   Passion unfolding in hundred year old parchments

They say she is quite ancient   A quiet agent ravaging thru villages of men

and leaving them in total confusion

For she leaves hieroglyphics scribbled on their hearts

Her mark   imbedded in their minds   a new religion

Worship   praise   admiration   and at times obsession

and at times obsession   But she is not oppressive

You can choose what you may   and she will continue to be who she is   as she is

Intentionally seeking your praises

And I knew right then   my standard of beauty

Would never be the same again.

*From Song by Shai-'If I Ever Fall in Love'

Artist Rendering-Picture of a Future Life

Her fingers walk playfully

Down

The

Line

Of

My abdomen

She's watching me   ever so carefully

Eyes beaming with pride at the physique of her man

Sleek muscles   Chiseled frame

"My Adonis", She whispers…

Kissing the "V" at the base of my neck…

Right hand continuing its journey along sable chest hairs

      Left, nestled underneath her chin   supporting mischievous thoughts

      I know that look   that smile which plots...

      Secretly seeking my innermost fantasies   fantastically reaching w/ so little ease

She's dressed in nothing but a silk bed sheet

      Revealing beautifully rounded bare shoulders   I smile

      Doing a quick observation of my brown skin goddess

      the mother of my ebony sons

      soundly stroking her man's ego w/ only bare fingertips 2spare

      & a whole lot of care....

I think of where we've been

      Seated in the hands of poverty   sinking

      Floods rocking us back n forth

      Planes penetrating our skyline

From sweat-filled days 2sleepless nights

Asking God 4better 2mrrw's   Imploring him 4mercies

Til we fell in place….

Fast-Forward   to you   me

& a multitude of concrete vows

In a jaded world

Attempting to exploit trust vulnerability & insecurities

My fingers walk playfully

Down

The

Line

Of

Her pregnant abdomen

I'm watching her   ever so carefully

     Eyes beaming with pride at the physique of my woman

     Gorgeous brown eyes   Incredible smile

     Round belly holding the life of my seed… & me,

     Kissing the "V" at the base of her neck…….

Carnival of Eve

Look at her. She. The only one present in the midst of a crowd.

Outstanding. Simply standing out while exerting no effort.

I love how God manifests His powers in the perfection of a woman—making believers out of double-minded men.

Look at her. She. Revitalizing the pages of an ordinary screen..you know what I mean—

Ordinary characters on a regular day, taking up space on a facebook page.

It's ridiculous really—how she can illuminate the darkest of days—the most mundane of things which are of no interest to me.

These fools—they see tail feathers—but I can see much better

Clearer in the sense that natural beauty is exuded

in more than just a "nice ass & tits" ,

is it a wonder why she gets so many hits?

Look closely & you'll find the *"It"* factor   In fact so glaring you'd be blind not to see it

Between her eyes & smile/ vision which can guide a man into the depths of Hell & right back unscathed…sure I know, it all sounds pretty insane….

Like Lazarus coming back to life;

I once held a knife to hand & slit the skin, only to feel the blood rush frantically thru my veins   feel pain surge up & down my arm and travel up inside my brain

That   is what it's like to know her powers

Blood

Rushing

Pain

Searing

And all at once

Crashing at a thousand knots splitting the atom

until ADAM is split…

How deep is your cut   Oh Eve

How strong is your power passed down from Him

That sin is just thissssss…   Thing.

For I will fight for you

I WILL die for you

I will lie in order to lie down with you   for you hold me up; in more ways than one

& if necessary, I will wage wars against the maddest of men whilst burning cities to the ground in order to meet your approval…   Oh Eve

That   is what it's like to know your powers

Blood

Rushing

Pain

Searing

And all at once

Crashing at a thousand knots splitting the atom

until Adam   goes mad.

lunar daze

I wanted to make love beneath the stars,

That's when she replied---"Noooo poet, now you're going too far".

I envisioned us beneath the full moon

being consumed by the eye of the celestial voyeur

sneaking peeks at us between lighting the paths of astronauts pacing its surface and soldiers heading to war

I wanted to make love beneath the stars

under a rain that would cleanse us

as we committed our dirty act with the purest of hearts

while mastering the lost art of embedding ourselves into each other's psyches

penetration beyond penetration

I wanted to make love

so that our movements could eclipse the lunar event taking place

& force nature to envy *our powers* for a change

I—poet, with scattered mind vast dreams   & outrageous imagination

devised a moment in time in which we were far from the foibles of this world, out of the grasp of our

foes & immune from the troubles which plague us

I wanted to make love-making an adventure again

that once forbidden pastime

like two juveniles—delinquent in understanding of the union

yet lusting after it with an unquenchable fondness

I wanted to make baby-making a planned course of action…

No contraception

cause the reason we were sleeping together was to multiply

& not simply to hide inside each other's arms, legs, go-betweens

& muffle our screams so the neighbor's couldn't hear us any more…

I wanted us to remember that what we shared

was nothing compared to how we'd fared in the past

cause that was the past

& baby we…you & I, are the future.

Chapter 3: Midnight in the Garden of Eden

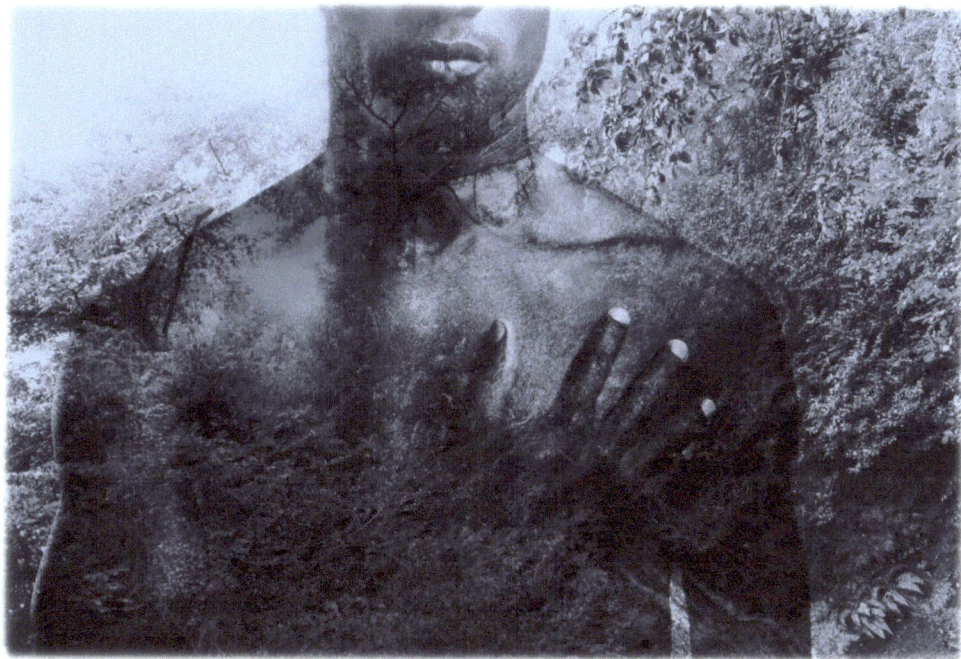

unity

touching her coyly with my member
I dismembered her thoughts
processes reflecting slivers of light hidden beneath the surface
at the core of things was

me myself n I

housed in the crevices of her body
open   to all three   we devised a plan to satisfy her urges   desires
it required great tact and observation
but we were   open   all three   prepared to fight   to entice   and excite
we were one that night   satiated was she   with me   he   and the last of the three

The Appetizer

My mouth fell just below her navel

      Her back arched

      hands over my ears

My tongue savored the smooth caramel

      I tasted her   dark & rich

      like sippin' on some secret Bailey's mix on a cool day in July—Sweet

My other senses grew jealous

      So I tied my arms around her waist

      leaned forward & drew in the chocolate scent

My eyes grew restless

      So I pushed back & allowed them to scan her frame

      inch   by inch

My ears protested the silence so I removed her hands

      She accepted my kisses

      & treated my eardrums to a symphony of moaning

      In the key of A…..

I drink her in slowly & she goes down smooth

Gently stroking   Formulating my thoughts

Spirit elevated Again rejuvenated

We are this **WEIRD** science

Charging each other like electric currents.

She vibrates, I awaken.

I am Mercury & She   Venus

She follows me well, but holds me up all the same.

THE BOUNTY

We   **Fucked like savages**

Ravaging each other's bodies in twilight

The Fight   of the Century

She   vs. Me   vs.

Uncertainty & Anticipation.

It culminated in orgasmic reverberations

From one room to the next

As we vexed the very walls which held us

& felt us

as we rammed our volitions onto it-

                                     forcing them to submit.

                                     I tasted her lips in short intervals

                                     Between hip thrusts & tight hugs

                                     She clung to my back with catlike instincts

                                     I think…

                                     this could be the beginning of

                                     a beautiful friendship

                                     beyond mere favors   **as we savor**

                                     the moments

                                     the minutes

                                     the countless hours spent devouring

body parts

 in all positions which shall

remain nameless

before it all became shameless

Besides, there are better things to talk

about-

like   her mouth on my rock

Or said rock in her sex

Turn the page & you will see me on top in

the quest

Her at climax   an animal in main course

This   true discourse between

human beings

Being   in total agreement.

Tucked away in the corner, the serpent can only look on….

Sexy Music

Her body was my instrument

    Hands working dutifully across her skin

    my fingers in compliance to her needs

    lips in alignment with her thoughts

I played her   gently   roughly

    Carelessly falling prey to her every whim

    notes slipping from her mouth into my eardrums

We played

    She scanned my chest & licked a pec

    I pried both legs & kissed her sex

    the gratitude I received was a bite to my left earlobe

Her tongue followed the onslaught

      & slipped into & out of my mind's eye…

      Then retreated down to the base of my throat…

To her call   I answered

      Descending

      Pressing my mouth below her navel

      hands holding the fullness of her backside

We played

      She & I making melodies out of ecstasy…

      We slaughtered silence that day

      folding inhibitions between our sheet music

      & fusing sheet music with our street music

We composed our favorite song

      From dusk til dawn

& conveyed the language of our ancestors

without ever having spoken to them

Rhythms in perfect union,

Voices in octaves high

The night that we devised

me & she   she & I

our very own

Sexy Music.

LOVE-BONE

She said, Fuck me..Do me..Don't tease me

Screw me

The Poet replies,

Tonight   First,

Let me make love to you in words

Let me Explore your body in contexts you have

never heard before

War & Peace United in the

Valleys of your Flesh

Mountains

Rivers

    they

        fall &

           part

with my comings on your breasts

I will make this rendition the text men

turn to before they spread legs

Drop their pegs into the ground

& oceans spew forth onto the sheets

This.. will be the Tributary song

The Tribal language that describes the

anguish raging within men's loins

This.. will be sincere

Painting the union of the dick with the

clit, not as vulgar, but so natural-even

nature must embrace the deed

Can you   feel me on these words as I draw strength upon your taste

Make no mistake *I won't make haste*

Licking   Sucking   Flicking my tongue across your skin in rhythmic motions

        Damn that mouth…what an awesome love potion   Coercing your spirit to

dance with mine- your soul to awaken from it's sleep   more alive than it will ever be

More & more & more it demands of me

And so I comply   supplying you with just the right combination of soft touch

w/animal lust   Brute admiration that leads us to fuck—up down *sideways*

prostrate   standing knee deep in the water   me holding your weight…

To be continued…

true religion

i loved every inch of her frame
from the curve in her calves to the feel of her thighs,
her eyes   rivals of diamonds cut perfectly through....lips the rght size, just the rght hue
her smile, the very complex that perplexes the sages, for ages...distraught..attemptng 2 explain the
riddle..
as others fiddle with their purses and wardrobes   she stands....
bare   naked... clothed....and beautiful.

and so i went in......thrusted her with the rage of a bull ,
penetrating her walls with so much emotion i 4got who i was   where we were   or how we got there
there in her room with shades drawn hearts pounding and the sounds of her moaning thru the nite   ....

i felt alive
her joy was my joy
her pains   mine as well
deeply imbedded 2her hips   her body n mine became one cuming n goings so heavily
immersed.....none could tell neither beginning nor end..
just the exit wound.

THE EARTHQUAKE

We made love beneath

 the moonlight

between the sheets

beyond the trees

above the earth   we rumble

Our thighs locked as Samson's locks

braided on the possibility tomorrow may never come

From sunrise to sunset

we explored each other's bodies… a heavenly host

of symmetrical points falling into alignment

as the ground shook beneath us

a raging battle against it's gravitational pull

as we pull one to another   far & away

into & out of this here universe of seismic forces

in want   waiting to swallow us whole.

/Pull Over/

I want you inside me she exclaims

    His head jerks right   caught off guard by the demand

Her skirt is lifted

    just above the knee

    but enough to see the fugitive

    she's been harboring thru the long car ride

In/side   me   now

    She whispers in broken syllables

    head cocked back against the seat

    her right hand beginning the job

Left, grasping his thigh

    Pull   she lets out

    Pull over

His eyes scan ahead & lead…..

    Right   just shy a grass field

    they stumble out in haste/undressing each other in the process

    kissing   biting   two spinning shadows

    they emerge from spying taillights

    until both figures hit the ground

He slips between her legs with urgency

    As if the sky were about to fall

    His thrusts are sharp   rapid-fire

    muscles tense   veins popping   her nails imbedded in his back he grunts into the night air   She moans onto green earth   index finger in mouth

she lets out a sound so piercing he's forced to cater to the cries

But she's fine

In every aspect of the word

smiling   ear to ear   beaming

satisfied   like the sensation of wine warming into cold bones

he collapses alongside her….

Electric Slide-*Rewind*

I slid my fingers thru your hair

& felt you relax at the touch of my hands

You slid your tongue

down

      the center

         of my collarbone

I thought it felt good   so I returned the favor

Slipping down the slope of your neck   watching pleasure hiss from your portals

I tried to undue your bra

but the straps were too stubborn

so I slid you onto your stomach

straddled you as skillfully as I knew how

& began to undue you

piece by delicate piece

I kissed softly from the small of your back

down

      to the curve

         of your calves

as you called out my name

I drew myself up

& flipped you over again

My mouth reached yours & we collided

two beasts   Hungry   Devouring one another

in a feast of great proportions

As I tasted your breasts I heard you moan when I bit into the brown of it

then sighed with the syncopation of a musician tuning his guitar

you pulled one of my fingers to your mouth & began an appetizer

I withdrew

lowered myself   & when you indicated readiness with your eyes

I slid into glory like the caged bird that I was

Provoking the sweetest melody these ears had never heard…

It was our first time

So you cried

We cried

at the savage beauty of the moment

because it was so pure   natural

because it was carnal   because it hurt

It made sense

you were locked not only to my heart now

but to my loins as well…

so when one exhaled   both felt the movement

Joined at the hips   thighs hands eyes

& now in the culmination of it all—soul & mind.

LOVE-BONE

Continued...

Wait/just a second- let me rewind before this grind is too much for some

Allow me to explain how we got here

He created the Rib that I gave to she

Providing the sustenance & timeless vitality   then we became one

Forever lost without the other

Wayward explorers always searching for more

And more & more it demands of us

*And so we comply   supplying one another with just the right combination of soft touch with animal lust   Brute admiration which leads us to---*you know the rest

    but do you know the in betweens

How she completes my sentences & I fill in her empty spaces No wait   holes

Those gaping holes only the mate possessing the key to the soul can enter & decorate...shit, did I just say decorate?

Not too many things can make a man use words like that.. but here I am about to seal the deal & out pours.....

I want to adorn your body with petals-fresh Rose petals of June surrounding you entirely on a bed of silk woven sheets

Where lips meet softly in the most intimate of kisses   followed by hisses that'll make even the snake crawl back into his hole.. leaving us holding morsels of sinful pleasures at the tips of our tongues

It is then, we have really begun.

So just   lay back   relax

And at the end of this poem

Your waiting....... Shall cease.

Chapter 4: Revelation of Love

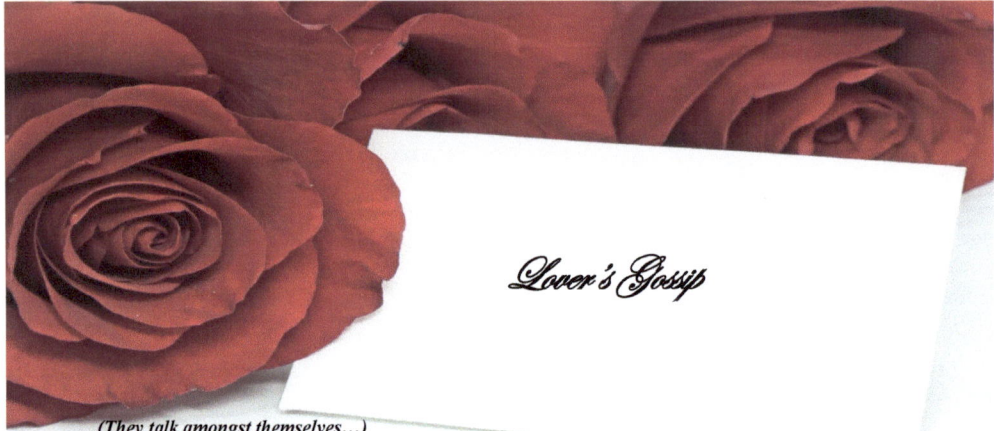

Lover's Gossip

(They talk amongst themselves…)

He says: The gravity of this situation is so heavy it leaves me light-headed

at the notion that we will be threaded & knotted as one..

..the warmth of the woman that God has intended/upended

The earth, the oceans, the stars

& has found no better rock for you to lean on than I

And in your eyes I see fire & passion which unites

Ignites the very fibers that make me a man

What is two? But one augmented to the other to bring completion.

Did I ever tell you that w/out you I am futile? A finite dimension, missing its layers

Yet w/you- I am powerful beyond imagination…

She says: You, who He gives in His own image- Imagine that- a demi-god,

Semi to no one but God   formulated to stimulate the woman who is me, for me- specifically

The protector lover of my curves as well as mind   Debilitating & all the same uplifting my

Sense of self- selfless, inconspicuous vessel @ my side

What is two? Did I ever tell you that w/out you I am fragile?

Breaking into pieces w/out reasons

I can find   A solitary reflection in want of light

Yet w/you-I am forever illuminated…

Le Jardin-"The Garden"

What pains me most is not that I've lost you

but to whom I have lost you to.

He doesn't see you as I do

flawed, yet perfect.

He sees you as a pragmatist does

With limited sight

Only the surface, missing the essence.

I on the other hand see you with the vision of a blind man

Unhibited in scope & reach

Every word you utter a treasure

Every minute a discovery.

He speaks with such dryness

when he speaks of you

his descriptions of joy *artificial*

& colored to gain popular approval

They find the applause of men

Yet leave you wanting.

Upon observation   he sees the flower

I see the very petals responsible for the makeup

So as we break up & you move on

to "greener pastures"

I ask only one favor

Remember me

When you discover the thorns in your lovely bastard.

Tainted Love-_The Corruption of Ryu_

The corruption began b4 I was old enough 2knw right from wrong-

& I learned 2accept corrupt men as part of reality-

But I could never accept them as part of the future.

She spoke   ...in regular beats   lacking emotion or concern

The artist in me decomposing under the weight of her words

  Eating through me like a terminal illness

  Flesh of my flesh, bone of my precious bone

  Ribcage ripped out like a tumor excised the wrong way on an operating table

She smiled   hiding her pain behind fixed porcelain

& it pained me to see how easily she could now lie   to herself

Engaging me in obstinate discourse of how my course was too sensitive

& her voice was more rational   And I bled..

Internally wounded by the death sentence she had just issued my heart- a now rotting organ simply serving the purpose of pump & circumstance

nothing more, nothing left.

No longer able 2feel, empathize,

or love with the right rhythms

And she… she can continue 2con herself into normalcy & normally that would work just fine but I gotta tell ya, just because some will eat pigs, doesn't mean we'll eat that shit. That shit about not needing 2b felt, touched, held onto or up on the highest pedestal   that'll just cause you 2bleed into me…Ryu..

The Corruption of Ryu could have been averted had there been more Jules 2save him. More Angels, Less Demons   distributing their vices in alternate shifts   & pitting his manhood against his good sense   & for just a few cents more he could get a pro instead of a preacher to come lay a hand on his head.

The Corruption of Ryu could have been averted had there been more Jules 2save him.

More Christians, Less Heathens   practicing preachings instead of practicing hypocrisy with 50cent condoms from the nearest gas station. And now, a moment for digestion….

Time.

She looked at him stoically   as he dissolved in her eyes into No-one & Everyman

who ever laid a hand on her body & defiled it   took by force w/out permission   or

pledged loyalty.. then gave her an insane sense of worship

She was like so many b4 her

I was just the temporary medicine

filling voids, absorbing hurts, & providing intervals of pleasure.

Yet still needing more than I could give.

The Corruption of Ryu began where she ended   where the rules could not be bended to accommodate

his sincerity

Where the truthful man was a foolish man   & his kindness a weakness

For one could not attempt 2mend a broken heart, but 4an ulterior motive 2defend... No?

But I digress.

This, is how it all began.

The Ex Factor

I think of you from time to time

Holding my thoughts hostage   you're like a thief brandishing a pistol overhead

I still see you

Sometimes clothed   at times naked

but always ravishing as ever

eliciting the most basic creature in me

yes I want to love   yet I'm forced to lust

So much time   So many years have lapsed & I stand

laughing at our foolishness…

letting society dictate how far we took the journey

I think of us from time to time

lying beside ourselves in carefree affection

your age is no matter   nor is mine

my youth is the appeal   your age is the charm

we mean each other no harm

 but still we exist on a plane that is set

& at times what we want   is not at all what we beget

I see your name in papers   stealing headlines for your skills

Your mind making matters of great importance seem like a silly pastime

I still remember the last time   you said goodbye & I drove away

half-hearted as we then parted

into a future which was unknown

Can't help but wonder if you too are in a storm

brewing inside your conscience

how we were so consciously aware of life

when we were near

I guess I just want to make it clear

in true poetic rhyme- you probably should know-

I still think of you from time to time.

Penis Envy-Her side

She says,

Sometimes I envy you.... walking around with the weight of the world on your shoulders

A proud man   a strong man

Trying to balance ego with sense & sensitivity

What I don't envy though—   is your penis—

He carries a slew of responsibilities in that package

Nations count on him to uplift & determine their fates

You need 2converse with the greats

After her monologues, your penis needs 2have a dialogue with my vagina

& get schooled in the anatomy of a real man- take heed n understand

Sometimes we don't just need a quick fix/   hit that, tap that, smack that ass…..& just walk away

We also need 2b kissed, listened to, talked to   ohhhhh so softly

with a *Hey baby- how was your day*

n how can I make it better?

Take this cheddar n help us weather the next big storm….

Your penis needs 2learn that some of these rap stars *are not his mentors*

But possible downfalls   Stiffen his stance/ be more enlightened

If   he wants to breed a bigger, better, well rounded…..   man.

He needs 2b schooled in the Art of Warfare

Not just in *Pubic* Relations, but also *Public* Affairs

Engage in Intelligent Discourse that can alter the course for falling men..

Serve as a means of prevention

B4 they become *"Priests" & "Scatters" who are <u>not</u> so "Fly"

B4 it's 2late 2even matter………

Old Man & His Sea

You are too strong for me now

ready to touch the sky before I can elevate my body

against the sands of time

I cannot hold you any longer

the way a tree cannot hold its leaves beyond a determined season

You are fleeting   fickle woman

& fight it I cannot

watching from the sidelines as destiny shapes your wings

preparation for the flight

Poised, in tune with the breadth of the vision

The scope of your challenge

But I cannot hold you any longer

As man is not fit to hold water in the palm of his hands

so I cannot contain your departure

You are too fast for me now

Quick footed   as a jaguar in pursuit of sure meat

Quick minded like a jackal evading her foe

slipping from my sight

I've got to let you go.

The Violins

Sound fuses thru night

Long & lofty

Strings are plucked

Fine tuned

Needle perfect

The players exhale cares

And commence precision in song

Sharp points of staccato melodies vibrate across the room

Into my mind

My third eye   no longer blind

Awakens

To a crescendo

Padded with a subtle vibrance

That sends chills

                    Down

                              My

                                        Spine

But wait a minute

I know this melody

I know not the song

But the crimson fox; bowlegged & sly

Rekindles a moment

When this rhythm was warm

Fresh & enjoyed by my lover & I

In a bottle of champagne

Surrounded by candlelight

Or was it the reflection of fire when I looked in her eyes?

Mmmmm, take good care of that violin, player

Cradle it   keep it

Possess it   let it speak thru the night

For you have no idea what will become of me

If you try & stop it.

The Graduate

on the road to completion...
She my thesis....

I studied her   as my cohorts
studied their subjects

She was my science- constantly rotating on a quite visible axis- yet I- never with access

On any given day   she displayed her magnetic pull
forcing both people & objects to *move* in her direction
This body   influencing the course of the stars
 I grew impressed   & so I left Mars
infiltrated Venus   devising the perfect plot to reach the core of the new planet
 in due time to insert my own slick chunk of granite

I drew up my own sandscripts to detail my findings
the kind you would find on the Discovery Channel-where one conjures hyroglyphics to leave a message
for a fellow mammal   carved with tooth enamel

She was my thesis   & through the desert I travelled to unravel her many treasures--of knowledge   of
bondage   or talents of body which could satisfy the id....

the atypical beauty

She had   no particular grace 2her swagger/ her walk slightly off beat

No coordinated movements which captured your gaze
No dimples, no eye twinkle that would leave you amazed

Her gait at times off it would make the onlooker feel awkward,
but you know, I gotta tell ya- regardless- I loved her..

Her hair was the shade of burnt amber in June
Not pretty, not ugly   nothing too special 2care
Facial features just average   skin not especially fair
but still, I loved her.

Her breasts were these A-cups that you could barely make out
Legs like two sticks of bamboo you'd use to bring a flame out
Lips not impressive, voice not seductive   & when she tried 2sound sexy   the
end result was often destructive,

but like I said in the previous verses- regardless- I loved her.

Somethin' bout those eyes of hers

When you look too deeply

It happens

Not quite natural

Like a mystique

Soft charisma piques the interest

All at once bold & daring

Leaping forth from portals

It has you caring a bit more than you care to

Soften up your touch

Is the message her lips deliver

Unspoken to his ear

There is no room for

Harshness here

…is there?

Word/Play

She speaks 2me in verses

    Words reshaping my manhood in powerful increments

    Dangerous verbs…explicitly woven with care...trickle from her succulent lips

    Sentencing me 2think with my other brain

Her body language instructs my next course of action

    Classical-this condition I'm in

    Dangerous curves   holding my eyes hostage

    As I pick my pockets for a proper defense

-If the ends justify the means, then I means to break bread with this enemy

    Keep her   closer than the average foe

She speaks 2me in verses

    Devising schemes 2 dismantle the walls around me

    constantly seeking my better man,

In a world where promises crumble, lies are abundant, & loyalty fleeting

    she sees that I remain.......

the martyr

Spanish Version

éramos más fuertes que la noche-
 pero a veces débil
comprensión en las razones para permanecer
el luchar para el rescate

éramos de gran alcance juntos-
pero a veces un obstáculo
el caminar a la gloria
entonces componer un infierno

rosas a las espinas
pérdidas generosas
un levantamiento de utopía
entonces quemando a las cenizas

tanto la amé-
Morí... para dejar que ella viviera.

Translation

we were stronger than the night-
but sometimes feeble
grasping at reasons to stay
fighting for redemption

we were powerful together-
but sometimes a hindrance
walking to glory
then composing a hell

roses to thorns
bountiful losses
a utopia rising
then burning to ashes

so much I loved her-
I died... to let her live.

NY Muse- Virtual Reality

I see your face   in pictures

The slideshow bandit   running rampant through the

concrete jungle I left behind

My mind plays tricks on me in pixels

Light particles crash against your skin &

features come to life

hair

nose

neck

chin

a life sized composition of humanity

humbling me

Cause you are virtually real

eyes

smile

arms

chest

I see you   but really I don't

watching through a thick man-made lens

as the extension of your body becomes one with my sensations

I see your face   in pictures

constantly illuminated   thriving in proportions

I stare… grasping at an intangible element

so elemental for survival it's fundamental to my being

existing only in the hopes of seeing you again

2mrrw perhaps in the weeks 2follow or someday soon

real soon…

& I think having a piece of you

is better than not having you at all.

Dia

We met on the first day of spring,

But see, here's the funny thing

I never really appreciated the seasons until that moment

moment in time when she

had me empowered

with the sense & sensibility

to approach & gain strength,

Scent of a Woman –

That's what it was

When the blind Pacino

convinced that dime to dance

except he was the one who taught her to *Tango*

wrapped his arms round her waist

& told her to follow

Yeah that's it baby,

I'll go where you go—

But I'll be the one who teaches you a new dance of life

The rhythm & tunes of an eclectic nature—

A vertical Kama Sutra of sorts

aborting the caged mentality that said we had

to be quiet about this sort of thing

Tap tap

Tappin' my way across your heartstrings

Showing you what it means

 to be appreciated & tasted in morsels

--much like the first day of spring

But see here's the funny thing,

I never really appreciated the seasons until that moment,

that moment in time when the

Flower enticed the bee & whispered

into his nostrils   come hither baby

come down & smell me

Yes, surely this is not

How the tale ends—but only the blooming

of a seasonal change

before the April rains come in to

devour the stench of her ill-fated past—

New beginnings you see,

Go tell her it's coming….   *(Stage left)*

And now,

Enter the bee.

I knew you before I   knew you

Really I did.

The crevices of your body being discovered by me for the first time,

But   not really.

Your touch, taste, feel beneath my hands/ for centuries

long before I ever set eyes on your features   cherry coated lips

calculating eyes

which hold me captive at night & devour my manhood,

I knew you.

Your thoughts, needs-your flaws even- I plotted the ways

I could correct you w/out offending, Uplift you w/out

appearing condescending or bending your wings so that you

could no longer fly, but instead remain dependent on my arms

For these arms are here to hold you- never to imprison your flight.

I knew you…

Not by name or by face

But everything else, perfectly in place…

from frame of body to state of mind

kind of like an outer body experience,

but I've experienced your being long before our bodies ever touched

The roughness of my beard against the softness of your features

The intricate pieces of you aligned with me,

The me being augmented & completed

Just by being in your presence...

I knew you...

Would someday find your way out of his dominion

to take me out of this darkness

this artificial happiness

where humans sleep with madness...

just for the sake of sleeping

I knew you long before I met you

& today,

I know you all too well.

Extensions

My woman is an extension of me

& I- an extension of she

we be the completion of the other one's puzzle

fuzzy thoughts run across the mind as I picture her navel

belly protruding

the vessel which carries my seed- my unborn child

of this… I am proud

for she is my other half & I have travelled a path

of great resistance & strong temptation

to arrive at this here destination

& yes, it was well worth it to make it out with my soul/mate & not just a bed/mate

to share the weak moments- but corny as it sounds,

I can spend a lifetime staring into those eyes

cradled in her smile

& though not impressed by her morning breath

I love the smell of her hair in the morning air/

Love to awaken to her voice with the morning sun &

corny as it sounds,

when she breathes- I / breathe

a sigh of relief that I didn't end this life when I had wanted to

because I wasn't sure where it would lead me to…

& she too has had this very same thought

as well as most the thoughts I entertain   she seems to share

Believe me I know it's rare cause yes,

my extension mirrors my poetic thirst for words that flow straight into the soul

& though the world may see this as madness—she understands an occasional outburst

in the middle of our lovemaking, sexing, freakin', smashin', or whatever the hell

people call it these days, but

I'd spit a Shakespearean twist like,

"Oh but soft, what light thru yonder pussy breaks—it is the east & her clitoris is the sun: Arise fair sun that I may bow…" To which my lady poet would reply in jest,

"Oh my good lord, I too wisheth to drink thee bone dry as thou doth taste of my marvelous rain."

And yes, we so comprehend/& no other man or woman could ever be so comfortable

with us—as we are—with us

so keenly attuned to the drumbeat—1 beat/of our hearts—we get lost

& say freak the world & their curses

Cause we have attained a finer blessing,

Better than great wealth,

Fame & large mansions—

Corny as it sounds/

We have found—

Our extension.

Jules Ryu Pierre

Pieces by Jules Ryu Pierre- Poet/Spoken Word Artist

With Strong West Indian roots the poet Jules Ryu Pierre was birthed on the island of Haiti in the city of Port-au-Prince. Raised in Queens, NY he picked up an affinity for both the written and the spoken word. His writings depict what it's like to view the world through the eyes of an artist. His debut collection Adam's Rib leaves his readers with a greater appreciation of the music of poetry as well as one of God's most potent gift to man- his other half.

He now resides in Atlanta, Georgia where he carves out his next collection.

Contact:

Facebook.com/julesryu

julesryu@gmail.com

www.ingramcontent.com/pod-product-compliance
Lightning Source LLC
Chambersburg PA
CBHW051234090426
42740CB00001B/15